Published by Creative Education
123 South Broad Street, Mankato, Minnesota 56001
Creative Education is an imprint of The Creative Company

Designed by Stephanie Blumenthal
Production Design by Patricia Bickner Linder

Photographs by: FPG International, International Stock,
and Tom Stack & Associates

Library of Congress Cataloging-in-Publication Data

Richardson, Adele, 1966–
Japan / by Adele Richardson
p. cm. — (Let's Investigate)
Includes glossary.
Summary: Introduces the geography, home and school life, foods, transportation,
and working conditions of the island nation of Japan.
ISBN 0-88682-983-6
1. Japan—Juvenile literature. [1. Japan.] I. Title.
II. Series: Let's Investigate (Mankato, Minn.)
DS806.R423   1999
952—dc21   98-12253

4 6 8 9 7 5 3

JAPAN

ADELE RICHARDSON

Creative Education

JAPAN
FARMS

Many Japanese farmers own three or four fields scattered around their village.

Right, views of Mt. Fuji and Tokyo

Japan, a long, narrow country in the Pacific Ocean, is one of the most technologically advanced in the world. It is also an old country rich with traditions and beliefs. The Japanese are a people who bring the old and the new together in their country.

*N*ippon, the country's name in Japanese, means "the source of the sun." Many Western countries have nicknamed Japan "the land of the rising sun" because of its flag, a red ball on a white background.

In Japan, a blooming cherry tree is a symbol of beauty and the shortness of life, because it blooms for only a few days.

5

JAPAN
FACT

You can stand any-where in the country of Japan and never be more than 75 miles (121 km) from the ocean.

Home in Kyoto, Japan

Japan is an island nation; it does not touch the land of another country anywhere. The country has four main islands—Honshu, Hokkaido, Shikoku, and Kyushu—and more than 3,000 smaller islands. Most of the population lives on the main islands. The capital of Japan is Tokyo; it is located on Honshu.

Most Japanese live along the coasts. This is because three quarters of the country is covered with mountains. Japan's highest mountain is Mount Fuji at 12,400 feet (3,779 m). Many of the mountains have dense forests. Rivers and streams flow down the mountains into the ocean. Japan's longest river is the Shinano River at 228 miles (367 km).

JAPAN
ROBOTS

The Japanese make some of the best robots in the world. They even have factories where robots make more robots!

Below, electronic circuit

JAPAN
FORESTS

*Japan is the tenth most **forested** nation in the world with 66 percent of the country covered in trees.*

Above, bamboo forest; right, snow monkey

The country is over 1,500 miles (2,415 km) long. It stretches north and south and is about the same size as the state of California. The winters in the north are extremely cold and harsh. To the south, the winters are much nicer, but the summers are hot and humid.

9

The weather is greatly affected by **monsoons.** They are strong winds that change direction when the seasons change. In the summer they blow in warm and moist from the east, bringing lots of rain. In the winter, cold winds blow in from over Asia and bring snow and frigid temperatures.

Mangroves growing off the shores of Okinawa

JAPAN
INDUSTRY

In 1980, Japan produced more cars than the United States; it was the first time ever.

Right, Shiraito waterfall near Mt. Fuji

NATURAL DISASTERS

Even though Japan is a small country, it is often threatened with natural disasters. One threat is from erupting volcanoes. Japan has 200 volcanoes; some can erupt at any time. Mount Fuji is a volcano. It last erupted in 1707. One good thing about volcanoes is that their hot lava heats underground springs. When the water forms pools at the surface they are called **onsen.**

JAPAN
GIFTS

Japanese cherry trees are famous all over the world for their beauty. The government has even given them as gifts to other countries.

JAPAN
SHAKES

Japan has more than 1,500 earthquakes every year. That's an average of more than four a day!

Haku Sansoro Garden

Earthquakes are another serious threat. Earthquakes occur when underground plates of the earth's crust slide against each other. Japan is very close to the edge of one of these plates. One of the worst earthquakes to hit Japan was in Tokyo in 1923. It caused a lot of damage and killed more than 140,000 people. Most earthquakes are so small they are hardly noticed, but Japan has learned that a big one can happen at any time. The country now builds skyscrapers that sway and absorb the shocks from tremors.

JAPAN

F A C T

Sixty-seven of Japan's volcanoes are active and can erupt at any time. That's 10 percent of the active volcanoes in the world!

E arthquakes also cause **tsunami**. Tsunami are giant waves. Many times they are caused by earthquakes in the ocean. The big earthquake in 1923 caused a tsunami 33 feet (10 m) high. These giant waves cause a lot of flooding and damage.

Japanese handiwork on display at the Battledore festival in Tokyo

Another threat comes from **typhoons.** Typhoons are storms that hit Japan usually around the end of summer. They are similar to hurricanes. The winds are very strong, sometimes over 100 mph (161 km)! They can move cars and even uproot trees. The word typhoon is Chinese. It means "great wind." Japan may be struck by as many as 30 typhoons every year.

JAPAN
F A C T

Japan makes two-thirds of all the electronics and computer chips sold all around the world.

JAPAN
WEATHER

During a typhoon, up to 12 inches (30 cm) of rain can fall in a 24-hour period.

JAPAN
FACT

Japan's trains are so crowded that the railroads hire special people called "pushers" who actually push people inside the trains. Sometimes there are so many people stuffed inside that the windows pop!

14

Above, a "pusher" filling a crowded passenger train; right, a woman dressed in Japan's traditional kimono

THE PEOPLE

Japan is very crowded. More than 125 million people live there today. If you were to spread all the people in Japan evenly across the country, there would be about 825 people in every square mile (or kilometer). The Japanese don't mind the crowds, though. They are very polite and believe that people should always be on their best behavior.

Most Japanese are **descendants** of people who originally came from Korea and China many hundreds of years ago. When the new settlers arrived, they found that people were already living in the land. These people, called the Ainu, like to keep to themselves. They speak their own language and have their own traditions. Today there are only about 15,000 Ainu left.

Japanese children by a prayer tree

JAPAN

FACT

Some Japanese nursery schools require an entrance exam, or test, for three-year-olds.

JAPAN

SCHOOL

Starting at 12 years of age, all Japanese children begin to learn the English language.

Right, schoolchildren crossing a busy Tokyo street; far right, child eating vegetable sushi

SCHOOL IN JAPAN

Japanese children are very competitive in school. Most kids enjoy going to school and would not even think of missing a day. Students start school at six years of age and are required to attend for nine years. Young people do not have to attend school after these nine years, but most go on to senior high where they prepare for college or a job.

JAPAN

Over 99 percent of the homes in Japan have color televisions.

18

Japanese schoolgirls painting in a park

School days are Monday through Friday and half a day on Saturday. To get extra schooling, some students attend **juku,** which is a school that teaches students a lot in a short amount of time. They may spend up to two more hours every day after school learning more. And that's on top of the homework they have from their regular classes.

All students must wear uniforms to school. One reason for this is to discourage independence. In fact, if a student tries to stand out in school, he or she will most likely be ignored by the other children. Because education is so important in the Japanese culture, almost all students graduate. Students who do not graduate bring shame on themselves and their family.

*There are over 222,000 acres (91,020 ha) of mulberry trees in Japan. The leaves from the trees are used to feed **silkworms**, which can produce over 44,000 tons (40,040 metric tons) of silk in one year.*

19

Left, young drummers at a festival; above, a silk moth

JAPAN

EDUCATION

Since 1912, 90 percent of Japan's population has been able to read and write. That number is now over 99 percent.

Isumago village

LIFE AT HOME

City homes in Japan are usually apartment buildings or modern brick or cement houses. An average home contains two bedrooms, a kitchen, a small living room, and a dining room. Country houses are wood and are usually a little bigger than city houses. All the houses have many electronic goods such as televisions, radios, and video equipment.

Most homes have heaters or furnaces, but in the winter many families spend time around a **kotatsu.** A kotatsu is a low table with a heater underneath. It has quilts around the side of it that people put over their legs to keep warm.

21

JAPAN
FACT

People in Japan who want to own a car must prove they have a place to park before they are allowed to buy one.

JAPAN
STORES

Some of the largest department stores in the world are found in Japan.

Below, wooden shoes to be worn inside a Japanese home

JAPAN
TUNNEL

The Seikan Tunnel is an underwater train tunnel that's 27 miles (43 km) long. It is the second-longest underwater tunnel in the world.

JAPAN
FACT

Half the fare, or ticket price, is re-funded to passengers of the bullet train if it is more than a few minutes late.

Hida Minzoku village

A traditional home has smooth mats called **tatami** covering the entire floor. No one walks on these mats with their street shoes on. In Japan, you must leave your outside shoes at the door and put on other shoes that are worn only inside the house. To keep the floors spotlessly clean, there are even special shoes that are worn only in the bathroom!

The Japanese like to rest and relax too. Each night the whole family takes turns soaking in a square tub filled with hot water. The tub is not for taking a bath, though. It is just for soaking, and people must already be clean before they get in. There are even public bath houses called **sento** that anyone can visit.

Since there is so little space in Japan, rooftops sometimes have gardens and even amusement parks with rides!

Left, bathers walking to hot springs in Kinosaki; above, a traditional Japanese lantern

JAPAN
VOTING

Japanese citizens are not allowed to vote until they are 20 years old.

JAPAN
MEALS

Most people in Japan drink tea and eat rice for breakfast, lunch, and dinner.

In most families the mother stays at home while the father goes to work. If the mother has an errand to run, or happens to work, grandparents take care of the children. Traditionally, grandparents lived with their children and grandchildren, but that practice is no longer common in the cities.

Seafood is a big food item in Japan. In fact, the Japanese eat three times more seafood than they do other kinds of meat. Usually rice and fresh vegetables are served with the fish—sometimes rolled up in seaweed and eaten raw. This dish is known as **sashimi.** Some people call it **sushi,** but real sushi can be made with cooked seafood or with no meat at all—just vegetables. Meals are eaten with chopsticks, a practice that originated thousands of years ago in China.

JAPAN
SHIPS

Of all the ships sailing in the world today, half of them were built in Japan.

25

Far left, sea bass for sale at market; left, sashimi plate of raw fish

JAPAN
FARMS

Most family farms in Japan are very small; many are only 2.5 acres (1 ha).

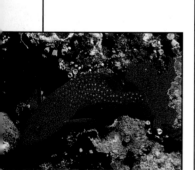

Above, red sea grouper; right, tea fields; far right, harvesting rice

Rice is also a big food item. It is one of Japan's biggest farm crops. Rice fields, called **paddies,** take up almost half the farming land available. The rice needs a lot of water when it is first planted, so farmers flood the fields. In the old days, farmers had to stand, bent over, in knee-deep water to plant the fields. Today they use farm machinery.

Fish farms are also common in Japan. The fish farmers raise fish in tanks or ponds and then sell them to the markets. The Japanese also fish in the ocean.

JAPAN
INCOME

Less than half the workers in Japan are women, and their average pay is half the amount of a man's pay.

Above, bullet trains lined up; right, Yokohama Bay bridge

TRAVEL IN JAPAN

Most people in Japan own cars, but they use them only on the weekends. Since there's not much space for parking, people take commuter trains to and from work. There is even a super fast train called the **bullet train** that travels between major cities. This train can go as fast as 130 mph (209 kph).

Another fast train is the **maglev,** which stands for "magnetically levitated." This train does not touch the track but hovers above it at speeds of over 300 mph (483 kph).

JAPAN
FACT

Above, capsule hotel; right, snow festival in Sapporo, Japan; far right, young girl in a traditional kimono

WORK IN JAPAN

The Japanese work very hard to produce some of the best electronics in the world. Often the Japanese work six days a week, with Sunday off to spend with the family. Some people live far away from the companies they work for and rent small sleeping spaces, called capsule hotels, near their jobs.

Japanese companies treat their employees well for their loyalty. Benefits often include inexpensive housing near the company as well as health care and two weeks paid vacation a year.

Over the years, Japan has set an example other countries can follow. Through hard work and cooperation, they have made great things happen.

Glossary

Bullet trains are fast trains that can travel at speeds of 130 mph (209 kph).

Descendants are the offspring, or children, of older relatives.

Land that is **forested** is covered with trees, or forests.

Juku is a Japanese school that teaches a lot of information in a short amount of time.

A low table surrounded by quilts with a heater underneath is called a **kotatsu.**

Maglev stand for magnetically levitated. It is a type of very fast train that runs above a magnetic track.

Monsoons are very strong winds that changes direction depending on the season; they usually bring a lot of rain or snow to the region.

Nippon is the Japanese name for the country of Japan. It literally means "the source of the sun."

Onsen are pools of water from underground heated springs.

Wet areas where rice is grown are called **paddies.**

Raw seafood is called **sashimi.**

Sento are public bath houses.

Caterpillars that produce silk, used in making clothes, are called **silkworms.**

A type of food made of rice, vegetables, or meat rolled up in seaweed is called **sushi.**

Tatami are smooth floor mats that cover the floors of most Japanese homes.

Tsunami (soo-NAH-mee) are giant waves caused by underwater earthquakes or erupting volcanoes.

Typhoons (ty-FOONS) are very strong storms with high winds.